CAR
MECHANIC
WORKING UNDER THE HOOD

CAREERS WITH EARNING POTENTIAL

CAR MECHANIC

CHEF

COSMETOLOGIST

DOG GROOMER

MASSAGE THERAPIST

FARMER

THE ARTS

—

PRESENTING YOURSELF

CAREERS WITH EARNING POTENTIAL

CAR
MECHANIC
WORKING UNDER THE HOOD

Christie Marlowe and Andrew Morkes

MC

MASON CREST
PHILADELPHIA
MIAMI

Mason Crest
450 Parkway Drive, Suite D
Broomall, Pennsylvania 19008
(866) MCP-BOOK (toll-free)
www.masoncrest.com

First printing
9 8 7 6 5 4 3 2 1

ISBN (hardback) 978-1-4222-4322-0
ISBN (series) 978-1-4222-4319-0
ISBN (ebook) 978-1-4222-7486-6

Cataloging in Publication Data on file with the publisher.

Developed and Produced by National Highlights, Inc.
Editor: Andrew Gance
Interior and cover design: Jana Rade, impact studios
Interior layout: Tara Raymo, CreativelyTara
Production: Michelle Luke
Proofreader: Abby Jaworski

TABLE OF CONTENTS

KEY ICONS TO LOOK FOR:

WORDS TO UNDERSTAND: These words with their easy-to-understand definitions will increase the reader's understanding of the text while building vocabulary skills.

SIDEBARS: This boxed material within the main text allows readers to build knowledge, gain insights, explore possibilities, and broaden their perspectives by weaving together additional information to provide realistic and holistic perspectives.

EDUCATIONAL VIDEOS: Readers can view videos by scanning our QR codes, providing them with additional educational content to supplement the text. Examples include news coverage, moments in history, speeches, iconic sports moments, and much more!

TEXT-DEPENDENT QUESTIONS: These questions send the reader back to the text for more careful attention to the evidence presented there.

RESEARCH PROJECTS: Readers are pointed toward areas of further inquiry connected to each chapter. Suggestions are provided for projects that encourage deeper research and analysis.

SERIES GLOSSARY OF KEY TERMS: This back-of-the-book glossary contains terminology used throughout this series. Words found here increase the reader's ability to read and comprehend higher-level books and articles in this field.

WORDS TO UNDERSTAND

diagnose: to identify an illness or a problem

engineering: the branch of science that is focused on the design, building, and use of machines and structures

fulfilling: something that is very satisfying and rewarding

intricate: something that is very detailed and complicated

technology: the machines and tools that are developed from scientific knowledge

CHAPTER 1

CAR CULTURE AND AUTOMOTIVE CAREERS

CARS AND MECHANICS: ESSENTIAL PARTS OF OUR LIVES

Most people could not do without their cars. They are more than just the way we get around. Whether we use them to commute (travel) to work, go shopping, visit friends or family, or just relax, we spend a substantial amount of our time in vehicles. In fact, the AAA Foundation for Traffic Safety reports that the typical American spends an average of 293 hours a year in their car. That's more than twelve days a year!

The motorwagen created by Karl Benz in 1895.

While many people are given credit for having had a hand in inventing the modern automobile, German engineer Karl Benz invented the first "*motorwagen*" in 1895. Ever since this groundbreaking invention, there has been a group of men and women who have become a necessary part of keeping the world moving: auto mechanics. Of course, these mechanics also work on trucks, buses, and other types of vehicles.

While Benz's invention led to the first people who worked on cars, the history of the mechanic occupation actually goes much further back than the end of the nineteenth century. As long as there have been machines, there have been people who fix them. Machines break, and they will do so even faster without proper care. Mechanics are men and women with knowledge of tools, engineering, and technology who build, repair, and care for our machines.

Since the spread of the automobile in the United States and in other countries, mechanics have taken on a special and important role in the lives of most anyone who owns a car. We depend on people in this career to not only keep our vehicles on the road but also to make sure that they operate dependably and safely. By repairing and maintaining a machine that the majority of people depend on every day, auto mechanics provide a service that many of us consider a necessity.

Working as a car mechanic is a challenging but rewarding career that requires a variety of skills. Advances in technology have turned cars from a collection of motors, metal parts, tubes, and other mechanical parts and systems into high-tech machines with electronic control units that oversee everything from the engine and transmission to the vehicle's interior temperature to a minivan's power sliding doors. Despite the skill required for this position, most auto mechanics, however, do not have a four-year college diploma.

Learn why it's a great time to become an auto mechanic.

THE COLLEGE QUESTION

"I wouldn't change a thing," says Lindsay Valencia, summing up her ten years as an auto mechanic. "I really like my job. And on top of that, the pay is good. Every time someone drives away from our shop with their car fixed, I feel good inside. I like knowing that I am helping people."

Lindsay began to consider whether or not she would go to college while she was in high school. "Both my parents are college educated," she says, "and they both did pretty well financially. When I was in high school, my parents and I assumed that I would go to college, too. Thing was, though, I had no idea what I wanted to study. I didn't really have any big career goals at that point. In my sophomore year of high school, though, the guidance counselor at my school asked me, 'If you could do anything with a million dollars, what would it be?' At first, I came up with all the answers—buy some clothes, go on a vacation, things like that. But he kept pushing me to think about long-range goals, something I

Becoming a fan of NASCAR
is a great way to learn
more about cars.

would really want to do with my life if I could do anything at all. My family had always loved NASCAR [the National Association for Stock Car Auto Racing], so I finally said I thought maybe I would want to build race cars. I loved cars, but I had never thought about working on them. After that, though, I had this little thought in the back of my head. About a year later, I took a class on automobile repair that my high school offered. That's when I realized this could be a real job. It was something I would really love doing."

Like most people today, Lindsay's experiences during her high school years helped shape her future. Many students by this time are old enough to begin to explore old hobbies or take on new ones. Both in and out of high school, young people are given the opportunity to learn about themselves and the world. But even though no two people learn and grow alike, as students

Earning a bachelor's degree is a good strategy for some people, but not all.

prepare to graduate high school, almost all of them are asked the same question: "Is attending a four-year college the best choice for you?"

This is an important question, and for many high school graduates today, the answer to this question is "yes." In 2016, nearly seven out of every ten students

TEENS AND DRIVING

Getting your driver's license is one of the most exciting events in life. But driving a car is a big responsibility—and it can sometimes be dangerous. The Insurance Institute for Highway Safety reports that teenage drivers are more likely to be involved in crashes than all but the oldest adult drivers. Here are some of the main causes of fatal crashes by teens:

It's very exciting to get your driver's license, but driving is a big responsibility, and you need to be very careful on the road.

- Driver error: Teens are more likely to make errors than adults— mostly because they are inexperienced behind the wheel.
- Speeding: Going faster than the speed limit is a factor in one-third of fatal car crashes by teens.
- Passengers: Every passenger a teen driver transports increases the risk of a fatal crash; in fact, just over 50% of teen passenger deaths occur in crashes with teen drivers.
- Alcohol: Approximately 20% of fatally injured teen drivers have blood alcohol concentrations of 0.08% or more (the legal limit for adults in most areas of the United States); of course, as a teen, you should NEVER drink alcohol, especially when driving.
- Night driving: The fatal crash rate of 16- to 19-year-olds is approximately four times as high at night as it is during the day.
- Low safety belt use: Unfortunately, most teens who are killed in vehicle crashes were not wearing their seat belts.

in the United States who graduated from high school went on to attend college, according to the U.S. Department of Labor (USDL).

While many people see earning a four-year degree as the safest—if not the only—way to be successful, there are many other ways a person can find a well-paying career. The USDL lists more than eighty high-paying jobs that do not require a four-year degree—and according to CNN, half of all college graduates are either unable to find a job or ended up finding a job that didn't even require a college degree!

The Wall Street Journal reports that students who graduated from college with debt had average debt of $37,712. This much debt takes more than ten years to pay off! So while earning a bachelor's degree may seem like the best way to land a well-paying job, considering every option is an important step before deciding what kind of career to pursue and how to acquire the skills necessary to be successful. These options include receiving on-the-job training, earning a certificate in college and training on the job, earning an associate's degree, attending a technical school after high school, working as a trainee, or receiving instruction in the military.

LEARNING OUTSIDE THE CLASSROOM

Lindsay believes that an education doesn't always mean sitting in a classroom—but an education does always mean that you're willing to learn. She explains why a college education was not the right choice for her. "It's not because I didn't want to improve myself. I always loved learning. I'm discovering something new every day. There is so much to learn about cars. The technology these days is pretty amazing. And it keeps getting more complicated. So that means there is always more for me to learn. People think that cars are all the same—but actually, there are about a million tiny differences between each make and model. You could read every book on vehicle repair and you'd still be surprised by how much you do not know."

Not only is learning an important part of starting a career as a car mechanic, but it is also an important part of being a successful mechanic. As the technology becomes more **intricate** and complex, so do our cars. Until recently, a mechanic's job was purely mechanical in nature, but now mechanics need a much broader base of knowledge. Cars have come a long way since the earliest models back in the nineteenth century!

"These days," Lindsay says, "there is always some new technology that's revolutionizing [completely changing] the industry. My boss talks about how back in the 1980s, there was a big rush to learn computer technology. Now that's just standard, because all new

DID YOU KNOW?

Toyota Motor Corporation reports that the average car has about 30,000 parts—ranging from tiny screws to tires to the engine block.

models since then have computers. When I was starting out, the new thing was hybrid and clean-diesel technology. I had to learn about electric cars. And they keep changing. I've had to learn two or three whole new electrical systems."

The automobile repair class Lindsay took her junior year of high school was a turning point for her. "I found out I loved everything about car repair. I liked getting my hands dirty, I liked working with my hands, I liked that feeling

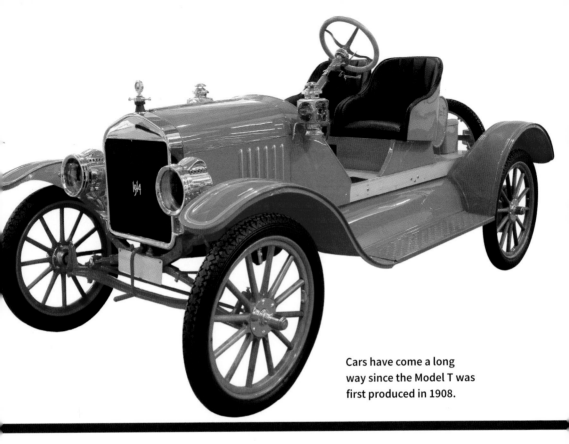

Cars have come a long way since the Model T was first produced in 1908.

you get when you suddenly figure out what's wrong with an engine—and you can fix it! I loved it all. I was so excited—it was like falling in love!"

When Lindsay told her parents how much she enjoyed her automotive repair class, they encouraged her to speak to a local mechanic, a friend of her father who had been working on the family's cars for many years. "He let me go to the repair shop twice a week and watch him work," Lindsay says. "He would explain what the different parts were for, and he told me how to use some of the basic tools. He explained the clues he used to **diagnose** car problems. When business was slow, he'd let me try out some basic repairs. He was really kind and patient with me, and never made me feel like I was just a stupid kid getting in his way."

Not everyone will have the chance to develop their skills in the same way Lindsay did, but her story makes an important point: Lindsay spent her free time exploring her interests and learning. She took time to become passionate about something. Eventually, that passion turned into a **fulfilling** and well-paying career.

"By the time I graduated high school," Lindsay says, "I knew I didn't want to go to college. My parents weren't too surprised. They could see how happy I was working on cars, and they just kept telling me they believed in me. So that's how it all started—and it's worked out well."

DO YOU HAVE A PASSION?

There's a lot of talk about passion these days: "Find your passion... Pursue your passion... Do what you love..."

Passion, it turns out, lives in all sorts of places. And while finding your passion is an elusive (hard to achieve) pursuit, there is only one real formula: Try things. Try things and see how they fit. Try jobs and find out what you like—and just as important, find out what you don't like.

The most important thing is, don't feel overwhelmed if you don't have a passion. Don't feel like there's something wrong with you. And then ask yourself, "What is something I enjoy doing? What is something I've done already that had aspects to it I liked?"

Passion can come later. Right now, just find something you enjoy. That's a starting point. Maybe it'll become that thing you can do for hours and it feels like only a few minutes have gone by. But don't put that pressure on yourself. Start small.

Adapted from the essay "The Truth About Finding Your Passion" by Colin Ryan. More of his work can be found at his website, www.colinryanspeaks.com.

Many people develop an interest in pursuing a career in auto mechanics by taking automotive repair classes in high school and college.

RESEARCH PROJECT

Talk to several auto mechanics about how technology has changed the field during the last few years. Ask them for advice on how best to prepare for this career.

TEXT-DEPENDENT QUESTIONS

1. Who is Karl Benz?
2. What is the average student loan debt for college graduates?
3. How did Lindsay learn more about a career as an auto mechanic?

WORDS TO UNDERSTAND

chain: a business with at least two, but often many, units

dealership: a business that sells goods or services for a larger company

fuel economy: the relationship between the distance traveled and the amount of fuel used by the vehicle

maintenance: the process of keeping something in good condition

specialize: to become an expert in something

CHAPTER 2

WHAT DO CAR MECHANICS DO?

TYPES OF CAR MECHANICS

Auto mechanics inspect, repair, and maintain cars and light trucks. Most mechanics work either for a **dealership**, where cars are sold, or for an independent repair shop. Dealerships usually focus on the repair and **maintenance** of a specific brand of cars—Toyota or Ford, for example. Independent repair shops either service all small vehicles or **specialize** in one portion of repair and maintenance, such as auto body repair. Independent repair shops can either be large **chains** of repair shops or local privately owned shops. While duties for car mechanics vary depending on where they work, the career of mechanic can be broken down into two categories: *journeymen* and *master mechanics*. Journeymen perform general tasks, such as maintenance, and they usually specialize in the kinds of parts that they repair. Master mechanics can repair virtually every part of the vehicle. In some cases, they specialize in repairing the transmission system—a very complicated part of a car that sends power from the engine to the wheels.

JOURNEYMEN

"All master mechanics start out as journeymen," says Justin Giambruno, a master mechanic who owns his own repair shop. "To get certified as a master mechanic, you need at least two years of experience as a journeyman—and a lot of knowledge about the different systems in a car."

A journeyman tightens lug nuts on a wheel.

When Justin says "systems in a car," he is referring to the connected parts of a car that work together to make a certain portion of the car—the brakes or the air conditioner, for example—do its job. The U.S. Bureau of Labor Statistics lists five different types of journeymen based on the kinds of systems they repair and the duties for which they are responsible:

- *Automotive air-conditioning repairers* install and repair air conditioners and service parts. They are trained in the use of refrigerants (chemicals that make or keep things cold) in a car's air-conditioning system.

- *Brake repairers* adjust brakes, replace parts of the brakes that wear down over time, and make other repairs to brake systems. Some technicians specialize in both brake and front-end work.

A brake repairer replaces the brakes on a car.

- *Front-end mechanics* align and balance wheels and repair steering mechanisms and other systems. They frequently use special alignment equipment and wheel-balancing machines.

- *Transmission technicians* and *rebuilders* work on gear trains, couplings, hydraulic pumps, and other parts of transmissions. Extensive knowledge of computer controls, the ability to diagnose electrical and hydraulic problems, and other specialized skills are needed to work on these complex components.

- *Tune-up technicians* adjust or replace parts to ensure that the engine is running efficiently. They often use electronic testing equipment to find and fix problems in fuel, ignition, and emissions (pollution) control systems.

According to Justin, when a journeyman works in only one of these areas, they are called a "specialty technician." However, it is very rare to find any journeyman who works on only one of these systems. "Most repair shops will have one or two master mechanics working for them. At my shop, the master mechanic owns the business. That's pretty common. But all repair shops have journeymen to take care of the small jobs, stuff like maintenance and helping out with bigger jobs."

MAINTENANCE

Maintenance tasks are much easier to carry out than a repair. That's because if the mechanic is doing maintenance, they don't need to diagnose what made something go wrong. Also, fewer parts are involved. Most car companies (known as automakers) design certain parts

OPPORTUNITIES IN THE MILITARY

Automotive and heavy-equipment mechanics maintain and repair vehicles such as jeeps, trucks, cars, and even tanks and other combat vehicles. They also repair bulldozers and other construction equipment. In the U.S. military, mechanics can find opportunities in the Army, Marine Corps, Navy, Air Force, and Coast Guard. Mechanics also work in the militaries of other countries.

A maintenance mechanic refills radiator fluid on a car.

such as air and oil filters to be maintained regularly. After a specific number of miles, all cars require certain maintenance, such as replacing the various fluids or rotating the tires (alternating where each tire is mounted so that it doesn't wear down as quickly) in order to prevent worse problems or even accidents while driving.

Other forms of maintenance occur less regularly but are still common. Parts such as brakes, batteries, and tires are not designed to last the life of a vehicle, so they will need to be replaced at some point. Exactly when these parts will need to be replaced depends on how a person drives and how they take care of their car. By taking care of routine maintenance, journeymen learn all the different systems of a vehicle, what purposes they serve, and how these different systems work together. They get valuable experience that will help them get better at their career.

FACTORY RECALLS

"Another kind of maintenance," says Justin, "is a factory recall." A factory recall happens when the car company discovers that a part installed on a specific kind of car is breaking often or is a possible safety risk. In either case, the company that made the cars begins a "recall," which means that the company either recommends or requires that an owner of the car replace the part.

"Only mechanics working for car dealerships have to worry about recalls," Justin continues. "I started out working as a technician's helper in a Honda dealership, so that's why I know about recalls. Some of them were a nightmare." According to Justin, any work during a recall is free for the customer—but for journeymen, it can mean replacing the same part hundreds or thousands of times in just a few weeks!

INSPECTIONS

While independent repair shops don't see any recalls, they see a lot more inspections than the dealerships do. In most American states, a mechanic with a good amount of experience and a special certification from the government is required to check or "inspect" every vehicle registered in the state for safety or emissions problems (emissions are the particles of pollution given off by things such as cars and factories).

"When you're doing a safety check," Justin says, "you make sure the tires are in good shape. The brakes work. The lights, the horn, the windshield wipers, everything—it all has to be working. You also have to make sure the car complies with all the standards that have been set for that make." When a journeyman inspects the emissions of a car, they have to measure the amount of certain

WHAT ARE ALTERNATIVE-FUEL VEHICLES?

Today, at least 250 million vehicles are on the roads just in the United States alone. That's a lot of gas—and a lot of pollution from exhaust. Researchers are developing more energy-efficient fuels and vehicles to reduce pollution and improve **fuel economy**. Some of the technologies that have been developed include the following:

Fuel cell vehicles: A fuel cell is a mechanical device that works like a battery but does not run down or need recharging. Fuel cells use the chemical energy of hydrogen or another fuel to cleanly and efficiently produce electricity. The National Renewable Energy Laboratory says that "these vehicles have the potential to provide pollution-free transportation as well as to reduce the nation's dependence on imported oil."

Hybrid electric vehicles: These vehicles often look like regular cars and trucks, but they usually have an electric motor and a small internal combustion engine (ICE). They are powered by two energy sources: an energy storage device (such as a battery pack) and an energy conversion unit (such as a fuel cell or combustion engine). Hybrid electric vehicles offer better fuel economy and produce less pollution than ICE vehicles do.

Plug-in hybrid vehicles: This type of vehicle features both a battery pack and a combustion engine that uses gasoline or another type of fuel. The car uses electricity for short trips and uses liquid fuel for longer trips. Unlike a standard hybrid electric vehicle with a battery, drivers can recharge this type of car by taking it to a recharging station or simply plugging it into an electrical outlet in their garage.

Biofuel-powered vehicles: These cars, trucks, and other vehicles are powered by plant materials that are converted into liquid fuels. One popular biofuel is ethanol, which is made from the sugars found in grains such as corn, barley, sorghum, and rice, as well as from sugarcane, sugar beets, potato skins, yard clippings, tree bark, and switchgrass.

Source: National Renewable Energy Laboratory

chemicals produced by the car when it is running. These chemicals could be harmful to the environment or to people's health. A journeyman has to hook up the car to a computer in order to determine the amount of chemicals that the car is producing.

An auto mechanic discusses a typical day on the job.

MASTER MECHANICS

Master mechanics also complete maintenance, recalls, and inspections, but journeymen usually handle these kinds of simple and routine work. Master mechanics are more likely to diagnose (find out what is wrong) and handle repairs.

"Repairs," says Justin, "can be tough. It's hard to figure out what's wrong sometimes." In some cases, according to Justin, large repair shops will hire a journeyman specifically trained in diagnosing car problems, but most repair shops are not big enough to offer this kind of position.

A master mechanic (right) instructs a trainee.

"This is where the master mechanics come in," Justin explains. "When someone has years of experience, they get really good at the job. Guys like that know what to look for. They've seen it all a million times, so they know what to check."

Once a diagnosis has been made, the car can be repaired. In most cases, a journeyman with the right knowledge will actually complete the repair, but the master mechanic will tell them what to do. If the journeyman isn't very experienced with a specific system, the master mechanic will help with the repair. That way, the journeyman can continue to learn and will be able to complete similar repairs in the future.

A big part of diagnosing a car problem is talking to customers to find out how the problem started and what the signs were that showed that the car needed to be repaired. What noises did the car make? When did it happen?

What else was the car doing (for example, going fast, braking, idling)? Talking to customers professionally and courteously (respectfully) is important, especially when diagnosing a problem.

Master mechanics usually need to talk to customers about a lot of things. They're the ones who usually communicate to customers what work was performed to fix a car and how to prevent a problem in the future. "Talking to customers," Justin says, "is a skill you have to have if you want to be a master mechanic. People who like their mechanic turn into loyal customers. They keep coming back. Some of my customers have been coming to me for years."

TAKE A PIT STOP

In automobile racing, a pit stop is when a race car stops during a race for refueling, new tires, repairs, mechanical adjustments, or any combination of these. Pit stop work is carried out by anywhere from five to twenty mechanics. This group is called a pit crew.

A pit crew in professional racing generally has nine assigned roles. A crew chief and a car chief are in charge of the pit crew before, during, and after a race. Seven other mechanics work on the car when it pulls into the pit lane. Five of these mechanics work on changing the tires as quickly as possible, while another mechanic refuels the car. The last person in the pit crew, known as the "seventh man," is responsible for taking care of the driver's needs.

Working in a pit crew is the most exciting and by far the most dangerous job that car mechanics can get. But with this fast pace comes a great salary of at least $75,000 a year, along with a certain portion of the money that the team wins by winning the race—a portion that can equal up to $150,000 for one race!

Working as a member of a pit crew is demanding, but also exciting and rewarding.

RESEARCH PROJECT

Ask your shop teacher or school counselor to arrange a tour of an auto dealership repair department. Talk to the different specialists about their careers. Ask them what they like and dislike about their jobs. Write a paragraph that summarizes each career. Which career do you think would be the best fit for your interests and abilities?

TEXT-DEPENDENT QUESTIONS

1. What are two popular specialties for auto mechanics?
2. What is a master mechanic?
3. What is a pit stop?

CHAPTER 3

TERMS OF THE TRADE

air filter: a paper or synthetic (made from chemicals) fabric part that collects dirt, dust, and debris from the air that enters the engine.

all-electric vehicle: a vehicle powered completely by electricity that is stored in onboard batteries; the vehicle is recharged by plugging the batteries into an electricity source while it is parked.

alternator: technology that allows a car battery to charge while the engine is running.

antilock braking system: a system on a car or other vehicle that prevents the wheels from locking up; this type of system can prevent skidding and improve driver control during sudden stops.

axle: a central shaft that connects to two wheels on a vehicle.

battery: a rechargeable component that stores and provides the electrical power that is required to start an engine; it also powers vehicle accessories, such as the radio, when the engine is not running.

biodiesel: a type of biofuel that is made from vegetable oils, fats, or recycled restaurant grease.

biofuel: fuels such as biodiesel and ethanol that are produced from corn and other organic products.

brakes: mechanical devices that slow or stop a car if the driver presses the brake pedal with their foot.

car creeper: a wheeled device that allows a mechanic to work under a car that has been raised off the ground; additionally, car creepers that look like a type of chair allow mechanics to sit while they work on the exterior of a car.

catalytic converter: a device that helps reduce harmful emissions from a vehicle's engine.

chassis: the base frame of a motor vehicle that supports the engine, brakes, steering, axle, tires, etc.

collision avoidance system: technology that is used to reduce the severity of or prevent an accident; these systems use radar, lasers, cameras, and sometimes Global Positioning System sensors to detect and alert drivers of potential dangers and, in some vehicles, take action (braking or steering or both) autonomously without any driver input.

combustion: a chemical process in which fuel reacts rapidly with oxygen and gives off heat.

dashboard: a panel of gauges that the driver sees when he or she sits behind the wheel; the gauges tell the driver how fast the car is going, how much gas is available, and other information.

dead blow mallet: a special type of hammer that is used to remove stuck bolts on car engines.

drive shaft: the shaft that connects the transmission to the rear axle.

drivetrain: the combination of the engine, driveshaft, differential, transmission, and axles that delivers power to the wheels of a vehicle; also known as a **power train**.

driving range: the distance a vehicle can travel between fill-ups of gasoline or electrical charges.

ethanol: a biofuel that is made from sugars found in grains such as corn, barley, sorghum, or rice, or from sugarcane, sugar beets, tree bark, potato skins, yard clippings, and switchgrass.

flexible magnet grabber: a hand tool that can be used to reach into engines or other parts of a car to retrieve dropped screws or nuts.

four-wheel drive: a vehicle system that can be activated when needed to power all four wheels of a vehicle; its purpose is to improve traction (the grip of the wheels on the road) during slippery road conditions and off-road use.

front-wheel drive: a vehicle drive system that sends power to only the front wheels of the vehicle.

fuel cell: a mechanical device that works like a battery but that does not run down or need recharging; fuel cells use the chemical energy of hydrogen or another fuel to cleanly and efficiently produce electricity.

fuel injection system: technology that sends gas from the fuel tank into the engine.

fuel tank: a container that stores gasoline until it is needed to power the vehicle.

hammer: a hand tool that is used to help loosen a stuck part, to straighten metal, or for other applications.

muffler: a device that reduces the noise created by the exhaust from a car's engine.

multimeter: a digital tool that is used to test a car's electrical system.

oil filter: a device that removes contaminants (dirt and other harmful substances) from a car engine's oil; if oil becomes dirty and filled with tiny, hard particles, the engine can be damaged.

onboard diagnostics II scanner: a digital device that allows the mechanic to interface with the onboard computer of any car manufactured after 1995.

pliers: a hand tool that is used to strip wires, grip or turn parts, or perform other tasks.

radiator: a component of a vehicle engine that transfers heat from the engine coolant into the passing airstream; it keeps the vehicle from overheating.

rear-wheel drive: a vehicle drive system that sends power to only the rear wheels of the vehicle.

rust: an unattractive and damaging effect that alters the physical appearance of metal on a car or other items; it is caused by a chemical reaction of iron and oxygen in the presence of water or air moisture.

screwdriver: a hand tool that is used to loosen or tighten screws, pry apart two pieces of metal, or perform other tasks.

shock absorber: a component that reduces the daily stress that a vehicle encounters as it is driven over bumpy roads.

spark plug: a device that starts a vehicle; it uses an electric spark to ignite fuel in the engine's ignition chamber.

speedometer: a device on a vehicle's dashboard that tells the driver how fast the car is going.

transmission: a component in a vehicle that takes the energy generated by the engine and transmits it to the connected wheels to move the vehicle.

wrench: a hand tool that is used to grip and turn nuts, bolts, and other fasteners.

WORDS TO UNDERSTAND

apprenticeship: a formal training program that combines classroom instruction and supervised practical experience; apprentices are paid a salary that increases as they obtain experience

GED: stands for general equivalency diploma; it is a substitute for a high school diploma for those who did not finish high school

manual drivetrain: a system in a car that moves the energy from an engine to the wheels of the vehicle

suspension: the system that keeps a car cushioned from uneven roads and potholes

CHAPTER 4

PREPARING FOR THE FIELD AND MAKING A LIVING

MANY JOBS, BUT MECHANIC SHORTAGES

"This is a great time to become a mechanic," says Rachel Borofsky, a newly trained journeyman who recently landed her first job as an auto mechanic. "When my folks were growing up, kids—boys, especially—started working on cars when they were teenagers. Most men knew how to take care of their own cars. They didn't need a mechanic for the routine stuff. Nowadays, it's a lot more complicated. Kids are more interested in computers than cars, I think. Anyway, a lot of people would rather not touch anything under the hood of their car. Fine by me! That's why I have a job."

According to Rachel, the fact that young people are losing interest in their cars is one of the reasons there is a shortage of car mechanics right now. Another reason is that more and more people own cars now—and as more people own cars, more cars will need to be repaired. A shortage of car mechanics means there are plenty of new jobs available for mechanics.

IS A CAREER IN AUTO REPAIR RIGHT FOR YOU?

"Not everyone likes working on cars," says Rachel. "It's hard work. You have to know your way around a set of tools. You have to be willing to get dirty. Sometimes you have to lie on your back under a car for a long time." Being a car mechanic is a very "hands-on" kind of job, and a lot of people don't like working this way. "Some people like showing up to an office every day," says Rachel. "I get that. But for me, this career is a whole lot more interesting. It's tiring, yeah, but it's also like solving puzzles every day. I'm putting something together, you know what I mean? And it's a cool job, really, because pretty much anyone can learn to do it."

According to Rachel, one of the most important questions that an interested young person can ask themselves is, "Is repairing automobiles right for me?"

She goes on. "Starting out as a journeyman is pretty easy. Somebody tells me what to do and when to do it. I don't have to take care of diagnosing problems. I don't have to figure out the best way to fix something. I help out with larger repairs, but I'm not really responsible for the job. My job right now

You can't be afraid to get dirty if you want to be successful as an auto mechanic.

is to just show up, pay attention, and learn. I figure that's the only way I'm going to make more money one day. If you want to be a master mechanic, you have to be willing to work even harder. You have to like a challenge, too."

Rachel doesn't plan on staying a journeyman for more than the two years of experience required to take the tests to become a master mechanic. "I am not sure that two years will be enough," she says. "People tell me you really need at least three years, and some people say you should plan on taking seven years before you take the test. But I'm impatient, I guess. I love it when I have a chance to figure something out."

Rachel's advice: Examine your strengths. "The best mechanics love working with machines," she says, "and they're good at solving problems. And you have to love a challenge." If you do, too, then a career as a car mechanic might be the right one for you.

WOMEN IN AUTOMOTIVE CAREERS

Women make up less than 2 percent of auto mechanics in the United States. This percentage is much lower than their share (47 percent) in the U.S. work-force. Reasons that women have "steered" clear of this field include the physical demands of the job, skepticism (doubts) from some customers that a woman can fix a car, and discrimination and harassment from male mechanics. Discrimination means not getting to do something or otherwise

There are many opportunities for women in the auto repair industry.

being treated in a negative manner because you are a woman, from a minority group, etc. Harassment can involve inappropriate physical or verbal actions that hurt someone physically or emotionally. Despite these challenges, a career in auto repair can be very rewarding for women. Some auto repair shops are becoming more friendly to women mechanics, and people are becoming more comfortable with the idea of female mechanics. A career in auto repair is rewarding for women for many reasons:

- No day is the same, which makes the job never boring.
- It's fulfilling to identify a problem and fix it.
- Once you gain experience, you can start your own repair business— which can help you make a lot more money than a regular mechanic.

Female auto mechanics advise young women who want to enter this career to try to find a mentor at their college automotive repair training program and/ or on the job. A mentor is someone who can provide you with information and support as you grow in your career.

Here are some organizations to check out that offer resources for aspiring and current female auto mechanics:

- Women in Automotive: www.womeninautomotive.com
- Women in Auto Care: www.womeninautocare.org
- Women's Industry Network: https://thewomensindustrynetwork.site-ym. com

Learn more about opportunities for women in the automotive industry.

BECOMING A CAR MECHANIC

There are many practical skills a person needs to become an auto mechanic. Many of these skills will be learned on the job. "But the best way to begin a career as a mechanic is to start working on cars as young as you can," advises Rachel. "The more you can learn on your own or from hanging out with people who are already good mechanics, the better off you'll be. After that, you might want to get an **apprenticeship** or go to a vocational school."

If you're interested in becoming a car mechanic, there are things you can do while you're still a teenager. "All mechanics have to have a high school diploma or a **GED**," Rachel says. "You can't just blow off school because you've decided not to go to college."

Mechanics need reading skills for studying manuals to learn how to repair specific problems or replace certain parts. You may also use math, and you'll

An instructor (left) teaches an apprentice how to repair a piston.

definitely have to work with computers. Most high schools have computer classes, which will help get you ready to work with the electrical systems of cars as well as the computers used to diagnose problems.

Some high schools have automotive repair classes that teach a young person basic auto repairs and maintenance tasks under the supervision of a professional. "No one wants to just open the hood of a car and start playing around," Rachel says. "If you don't know what you are doing, you could hurt the car—or yourself." Some communities now have technical high schools where young people learn auto repair skills while taking the classes required for a high school diploma. Programs offered by organizations such as the ASE Education Foundation provide educational classes and resources to high schools or groups of interested young people.

Vocational schools, which are also known as technical schools, are another great alternative to college for people who are interested in becoming mechanics.

Vocational schools offer training in a specific set of skills for a specific industry. These programs are much shorter than degree programs at colleges, generally between six months and two years, and they are much less expensive than college. "My technical school," says Rachel, "lasted a little less than a year—and it only cost me a few thousand dollars. I worked as a waitress to pay for it. When I finished, the school helped me find the job that I have now. I finished free of debt [money owed]. And I have a great job."

Though they are less and less common, especially in certain countries, another way to enter the automotive field is to get an apprenticeship. Automotive apprentices may begin with very little experience in car mechanics,

It's important to take as many computer science classes as possible in high school because mechanics use computers daily on the job.

but a repair shop hires them in order to teach them what they need to know on the job. Apprenticeships usually last longer than a program at a vocational school—about four years—and they sometimes involve classes in engineering and advanced automotive repair at community colleges. During each year in a U.S. program, trainees complete 2,000 hours of on-the-job training and 144 hours of related classroom instruction. Entry requirements vary by program, but there are typical requirements:

- Minimum age of eighteen (in Canada and some other countries, the minimum age is sixteen)
- High school education
- One year of high school algebra
- Qualifying score on an aptitude test
- Drug-free (illegal drugs)

No matter how you get the skills that you need, the small investment of time and money compared to the amount typically spent on a four-year college education means that pretty much anyone can be qualified for an exciting career as a car mechanic.

HOW MUCH CAN I EARN?

How much an auto mechanic makes depends on how much training or experience they have, where they live, and how many different kinds of repair and maintenance work they know how to handle. For someone who becomes a mechanic through an apprenticeship or a vocational school, how much they are paid depends, in part, on how well and how quickly they can learn to work with all of the different systems in a car.

It can be very rewarding to own an auto repair shop.

HIGH-LEVEL EARNINGS

"If you want to earn a big salary," says Alex McRaniels, "you have to learn fast, work fast, and get certified." Alex has been a master mechanic for more than ten years. He lives and works in Alaska, the state where mechanics are paid the most on average. When he says "get certified," he means becoming certified as a technician who is experienced and capable of repair and maintenance of different automobile systems. Getting certified in all the systems in light cars and trucks means that you have been awarded the status of a master mechanic.

You need to pass eight tests in order to become a master mechanic, but you cannot take any of these tests without at least two years of experience as a journeyman. These tests, given by a group called the ASE (the National Institute for Automotive Service Excellence), are to prove your knowledge and ability to repair these aspects of a car: engines, automatic transmissions, **manual drivetrains**, **suspension** and steering systems, brakes, electrical systems, heating and air conditioning, and engine performance.

"Once you have passed all of the ASE tests," Alex says, "you have to get recertified every five years. The recertification tests aren't as long as when you take them the first time. But you can't afford to get too rusty in an area. If you do, you could lose your master status."

In other words, a mechanic can never stop learning! But certification as a master mechanic gives you access to better job opportunities and higher wages. You will be able to oversee less-experienced mechanics and technicians. Some master mechanics, like Justin from Chapter 2, choose to open their own shops, which may allow them to make more money.

Master mechanics who own their own shops certainly make the most money of all mechanics, but they also function as business owners. This means they have many responsibilities outside of maintaining and repairing cars. Depending on the size of the shop, almost all master mechanics hire other master mechanics and journeymen to do much of the repair work for them.

Alex, on the other hand, decided not to open up his own shop. He enjoys his career as a master mechanic. "I make great money," he says. "I don't see why I would want to worry myself with owning a business."

Like most highly skilled and highly experienced car mechanics, Alex makes a certain portion of the money that the customer is charged for labor (the work that is done), also called a commission. This means that the more he works, the more money he makes. Alex works for a Ford dealership—and he makes $61,000 dollars a year, which means, according to the Bureau of Labor Statistics, that he is a part of the 20 percent of all mechanics who earn more than $60,000 a year.

AVERAGE SALARIES

Salaries like Alex's are possible for any mechanic who is willing to obtain experience, get certified, and take on the responsibilities of working at the head of a team of mechanics. But Alex makes a high salary for a car mechanic who has not opened his own business.

The average car mechanic in the United States makes nearly $43,000 a year.

SALARIES FOR AUTO BODY REPAIRERS BY U.S. STATE

Earnings for auto body repairers vary by state based on demand and other factors. Here are the five states where employers pay the highest average salary and the states in which employers pay the lowest salaries.

Highest Average Salaries:	Lowest Average Salaries:
1. Alaska: $61,410	1. West Virginia: $37,520
2. Washington: $54,420	2. Oklahoma: $38,750
3. Maryland: $53,770	3. Arkansas: $39,400
4. Hawaii: $53,520	4. South Carolina: $40,410
5. Michigan: $51,520	5. South Dakota: $40,440

Source: U.S. Department of Labor

The average car mechanic makes almost $43,000 dollars a year. But, says Alex, "When you consider all of the guys who don't get certified, stay stuck as journeymen, and don't challenge themselves to work harder or learn more, that number could probably be a lot higher." Alex was already making about $39,000 a year only three years after taking his first job.

Repairing and maintaining cars and light vehicles is a rewarding career, but it is also challenging. For some people, no amount of money would be enough to compensate them for working with machines every day. But for the men and women who have the kind of determined, problem-solving personality that being a mechanic requires, the pay is just a small bonus for the fulfillment (satisfaction) that they get from this work. Repairing and maintaining automobiles is a fantastic and well-paying option for anyone who enjoys this kind of work.

RESEARCH PROJECT

Interview auto mechanics who prepared for the field via on-the-job training, an apprenticeship, and vocational school. Ask them to list what they liked and disliked about their training method. Write a report that summarizes the pros and cons, and give a presentation to your shop class.

TEXT-DEPENDENT QUESTIONS

1. Why do mechanics need to be detail-oriented?
2. What is an apprenticeship?
3. What are the benefits of becoming certified?

WORDS TO UNDERSTAND

candidate: a person who is trying to be or is being considered for something, such as a job

entry-level job: one that requires only basic skills

ethnic group: a collection of people who have a shared connection based on their homeland, cultural heritage, history, ancestry, language, or other factors

soft skills: personal abilities that people need to develop to be successful on the job—communication, work ethic, teamwork, decision-making, positivity, time management, flexibility, problem-solving, critical thinking, conflict resolution, and other skills and traits

CHAPTER 5

KEY SKILLS AND METHODS OF EXPLORATION

WHAT ALL CAR MECHANICS NEED

While a passion for technology might make someone a good **candidate** for a career in auto repair, a car mechanic needs other skills as well, including **soft skills**. The U.S. Bureau of Labor Statistics lists six important qualities that every car mechanic should have.

CUSTOMER SERVICE SKILLS

Mechanics must discuss automotive problems—along with options for fixing them—with their customers. Because self-employed workers depend on repeat clients for business, they must be courteous, good listeners, and ready to answer customers' questions.

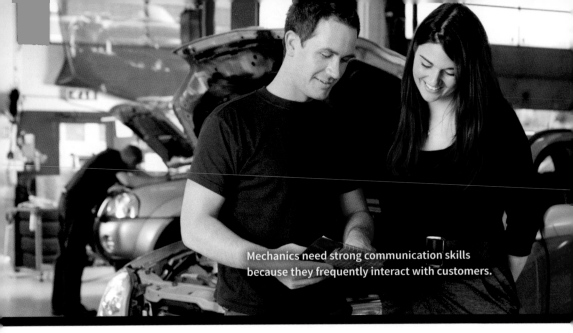

Mechanics need strong communication skills because they frequently interact with customers.

A DETAIL-ORIENTED PERSONALITY

Mechanical and electronic malfunctions are often due to misalignments or other easy-to-miss reasons. Service mechanics must, therefore, account for such details when inspecting or repairing engines and components.

DEXTERITY

Many tasks that journeymen do, such as taking apart engine parts, connecting or attaching components, and using hand tools, require a steady hand and good hand–eye coordination.

MECHANICAL SKILLS

Mechanics must be familiar with engine components and systems and know how they interact with each other. They must often take apart major parts for repairs and be able to put them back together properly. As a result, they need excellent hand-eye coordination.

TECHNICAL SKILLS

Mechanics use complex diagnostic equipment on engines, systems, and components. They must be familiar with electronic control systems and the appropriate tools needed to fix and maintain them.

TROUBLESHOOTING ABILITY

Mechanics must be able to identify and fix problems in increasingly complicated mechanical and electronic systems.

ADDITIONAL SKILLS

Car mechanics need a diverse (a wide variety) set of skills in order to be successful, but there is one more skill that, according to Rachel, is just as important as any of these skills. "Any good mechanic needs patience," Rachel says. "I watch the

Mechanics need excellent hand-eye coordination.

guys who are really good at this. They can troubleshoot just about anything without getting frustrated or angry. I really respect them. Customers aren't always nice either—but my boss never loses his cool. He's always respectful, even when they're yelling at him. He has this knack for calming people down."

Practicing patience in your everyday life is one good way to prepare for being a mechanic. There are also a number of other skills you can begin to practice, no matter what field you end up in. All employers need workers who are dependable (reliable and trustworthy) and responsible (doing what you say you will do). People need to know they can count on you. Every employer also wants workers who have a positive attitude, because positive people will not be discouraged by a challenge. And since for most **entry-level jobs** you'll work under the supervision of one or many people more experienced than you are, you also need to be able to work as a team and to take direction. Another aspect of being part of a team is the ability to work with people of different ages, genders, or religious backgrounds, or those from different **ethnic groups**. Successful mechanics need to move beyond these differences and connect with others in order to become an effective team.

If you already have some of these skills, you're well on your way to a successful career as a car mechanic. If you are not very strong in some of these areas, then now is the time to begin to learn and explore.

EXPLORING CARS AND AUTO REPAIR AS A STUDENT

There are many ways to learn more about cars, auto repair, and careers in the field. Here are some popular methods of exploration.

Museums, such as the Volo Auto Museum in Volo, IL, are excellent places to learn about cars.

ATTEND A CAR SHOW OR VISIT AN AUTO MUSEUM

At car shows, people get together to show off their antique cars or new cars that they've modified (e.g., by installing decorative hubcaps, raising the height of the car, painting the vehicle with vivid colors, etc.). You should attend one of these shows to learn about the different types of cars and get a peek under the hood. You'll find that people who bring their cars to auto shows love talking about their vehicles. Talking with car aficionados (someone who has a strong love for something) provides a great introduction to the world of automobiles.

You should also visit auto museums to learn about the history of cars and trucks and see vehicles of all types. For example, at the Volo Auto Museum, which is located in a northwest suburb of Chicago, you can tour more than thirty exhibits in twelve buildings on 35 acres (14.164 hectares), plus many outdoor exhibits. You can even see movie cars such as the *Back to the Future* car, the Scooby-Doo Mystery Machine, several Batman cars, and more than forty other

The "Git-Tar" car is just one of many specialty vehicles visitors can view at the Volo Auto Museum in Volo, IL.

movie and celebrity cars. At the California Automobile Museum in Sacramento, California, you can view 130 vehicles and rotating and special exhibits. Each month, you can even take a ride (with your parents, of course) in a 1931 Ford Model A or other antique cars. If you live in or near a big city, there's a good chance that there's an auto museum or car show nearby. Contact local auto associations to learn more.

ATTEND AN AUTO REPAIR SUMMER CAMP

Attending a summer camp is a great way to learn more about auto repair. High schools, colleges, community groups, auto clubs, and other organizations offer summer auto repair camps or workshops. Your shop teacher or school counselor can direct you toward camps in your area, or you can find opportunities by doing a keyword search on the internet.

Here are a few examples of well-known camps in the United States. Camps are also available in other countries.

Long Lake Camp Adventures

Long Lake Camp Adventures in Dobbs Ferry, New York, offers an Automotive Camp in which young people aged nine to sixteen work on classic American cars. They do everything from changing oil to replacing entire engines. Learn more at www.longlakecampadventures.com/automotive.

Universal Technical Institute

Universal Technical Institute (UTI) offers the three-week Summer Ignite Program, which trains high school juniors in automotive, diesel, motorcycle, and collision repair mechanical technology. The program is free, and students can earn academic credit that can be used if they enroll at UTI after they graduate from high school. The Summer Ignite Program is available in Arizona, California, Florida, Illinois, Massachusetts, New Jersey, North Carolina, Pennsylvania, and Texas. Learn more at www.uti.edu/programs/ignite.

Camp Motorsport

Camp Motorsport in Clover, Virginia, is a summer camp for girls and boys aged nine to seventeen. In this program, you'll learn how to drive a go-kart or off-road buggy in a racing environment. Learn more at www.campmotorsport.org.

Learn what happens during an automotive service competition at SkillsUSA.

PARTICIPATE IN A COMPETITION

Competing in an automotive repair or building contest is a good way to develop and test your skills. It's also an excellent way to make new friends and build your personal and professional network (a group of people you know who can help you get a job or meet other life goals). Regional, national, or international associations, corporations, schools, and other organizations car sponsor competitions. Check out the following competitions:

The National Automotive Technology Competition

The National Automotive Technology Competition is held each year at the New York International Auto Show. High school teams from around the United States participate in state- and regional-level contests to determine the top students from each location. The competition takes place over two days. On day one, contestants are tested on their knowledge of tools, measuring instruments,

A judge evaluates a student during an automotive skills competition.

specific vehicle components, and job interview skills. On day two, each two-person student team must diagnose and repair a number of preassigned problems under a car's hood in a certain amount of time. In a recent year, more than $3 million in prizes and scholarships were awarded to participating students and schools. Learn more at www.nationalautotechcompetition.com.

Skills Compétences Canada

Skills Compétences Canada is a nonprofit organization that seeks to encourage Canadian youth to pursue careers in the skilled trades and technology sectors. Its National Competition allows young people to participate in more than forty skilled trade and technology competitions, including Autobody Repair, Automotive Service, Car Painting, Welding, and Electronics. Learn more at http://skillscompetencescanada.com/en/skills-canada-national-competition.

SkillsUSA

SkillsUSA is a national membership organization for middle school, high school, and college students who are preparing for careers in technical, trade, and skilled service occupations. Some of its competitions that will be of interest to aspiring auto mechanics include Automobile Maintenance and Light Repair, Automotive Refinishing Technology, Automotive Service Technology, Collision Repair Technology, Motorcycle Service Technology, and Welding. SkillsUSA works directly with high schools and colleges, so ask your school counselor or teacher if it is an option for you. Learn more at www.skillsusa.org.

The Junior Solar Sprint Car Competition

The Junior Solar Sprint Car Competition is sponsored by the Technology Student Association and the U.S. Army Educational Outreach Program. In this competition, student teams in grades 5 through 8 compete to design, build,

A teen competes during the Junior Solar Sprint Car Competition.

and race the fastest and best-crafted solar vehicle. Learn more at www.usaeop. com/program/jss.

The Shell Eco-marathon

In the Shell Eco-marathon, student teams from around the world compete to design, build, test, and drive ultra-energy-efficient vehicles. Recent competitions were held in Sonoma, California; London, United Kingdom; Detroit, Michigan; and Singapore. Participants must be high school students and have a driver's license. Learn more at www.shell.com/energy-and-innovation/shell-ecomarathon.html.

DO SOME MAINTENANCE AND REPAIRS!

You don't have to wait until college to get experience working on cars. You can begin right now by doing simple repairs and maintenance tasks. Work with your mom or dad on the following tasks.

- Check and refill the windshield washer, oil, power steering, and brake fluids
- Check the condition and tension of belts and hoses

- Locate and check the air and oil filters
- Check the condition of the tires and the tire pressure

YouTube is a good source of how-to videos. Also, check out the following books for some tips: *Auto Repair and Maintenance: Easy Lessons for Maintaining Your Car So It Lasts Longer* by Dave Stribling, and *Auto Upkeep: Maintenance, Light Repair, Auto Ownership, and How Cars Work* by Michael E. Gray and Linda E. Gray.

SOURCES OF ADDITIONAL EXPLORATION

Contact the following organizations for more information on education and careers in auto repair, certification, and membership:

ASE Education Foundation (United States)
www.aseeducation.org/ase-education-foundation

Automotive Service Association (United States)
https://asashop.org

Motor Trades Association of Australia
www.mtaa.com.au

National Automobile Dealers Association (United States)
www.nada.org

National Institute for Automotive Service Excellence (United States)
www.ase.com

Renewable Fuels Association (United States)
www.ethanolrfa.org

Retail Motor Industry Federation (United Kingdom)
www.rmif.co.uk

Society of the Irish Motor Industry
www.simi.ie

INTERVIEW OR JOB SHADOW AN AUTO MECHANIC

Information interviews with a mechanic or auto repair shop owner are an excellent way to learn more about careers in the field. An information interview is simply a conversation in which you ask questions to learn more about a topic. Here are some questions to ask during the interview:

- Can you tell me about a day in your life on the job?
- What kinds of tools and equipment do you use on the job?
- How do you stay safe on the job?
- What are the most important personal and professional qualities for auto mechanics? Business owners?
- What do you like best and least about your job?
- What is the future employment outlook for auto mechanics? How is the field changing?
- What can I do now to prepare for the field?

Job shadowing takes the information interview concept a step further because you will actually be on-site to observe mechanics as they do their jobs. There's really no better way to learn about a career than to watch people doing it.

Car repair chains, professional associations, and youth organizations, such as Junior Achievement, offer information interviews and job shadowing experiences. Contact these organizations directly, or ask your school counselor or shop teacher for help. Additionally, ask your family auto mechanic to participate in an interview or a job shadowing experience.

A teenager removes lug nuts on a car.

RESEARCH PROJECT

Work with your shop teacher to create a combination career day/auto repair competition at your school. Ask mechanics from local shops to come and discuss their careers and judge the contest.

TEXT-DEPENDENT QUESTIONS

1. Why is it important for mechanics to have good customer service skills?
2. What can you learn at an automotive summer camp?
3. What is job shadowing?

It's never too early to begin learning about a career in auto repair. This teen was able to don some overalls and do some basic tasks during her visit to an auto shop.

WORDS TO UNDERSTAND

compatible: two things that work well together

hybrid car: a car that is fueled by at least two types of power, such as gasoline and electricity

vehicle emissions: the amount of environmentally harmful chemicals that are produced by a car or truck and released into the atmosphere

CHAPTER 6

LOOKING TO THE FUTURE

CHANGING SKILL SETS

The skills required for automotive repair and maintenance are changing quickly. Just twenty-five years ago, mechanics would have had a very different set of skills and knowledge than they do today. The future of the automotive industry is in highly technical and computerized cars that will need highly skilled mechanics to repair and maintain them. But while car mechanics will need a greater base of skills and knowledge to continue to be successful and advance in their careers, one thing they still won't need is a four-year college degree.

NEW TECHNOLOGIES, NEW SKILLS

"Today, your car can have as many as fifty microprocessors [small computers] controlling everything from emissions to safety," says Jada Edwards, an automotive engineer who designs engine components for a car manufacturer.

DRIVING WITH YOUR BRAIN

The Discovery Channel News reported that researchers at Freie Universität Berlin, a university in Germany, are working on a device that will allow a driver to drive a car with their mind. The device is called Brain Driver and involves a driver taking courses beforehand to learn how to tell the computer to turn right rather than left, for example. While Brain Driver has been completed and is currently being tested, we won't see this particular application in any new cars for at least a few years. But imagine all the new skills a mechanic will have learned by the time a customer comes in to complain that their Brain Driver isn't working and they have to use the steering wheel instead!

Automotive engineers are working hard to reduce harmful vehicle emissions.

In recent years, governments have become concerned about the high levels of **vehicle emissions** that are being released into the environment. As a result, manufacturers today have made computers a standard part of every car they produce. As governments have started making regulations (rules) that control the amount of emissions a car can produce, microprocessors have become standard. One of the best ways to reduce the amount of emissions produced by an engine is by carefully controlling the amount of air that is available when fuel is used by the car. Controlling this involves very precise measurements that only a computer is able to make.

Other examples of new technologies that are drastically changing the skill set needed by our mechanics today are electric and **hybrid cars**. Hybrid cars use a combination of at least two types of power to improve the distance they can travel with a certain amount of fuel. This means that a car's engine system and electric system need to work together in order to make the car move, and making these two systems **compatible** can be a large job for modern mechanics.

Electric cars are just one type of alternative-fuel vehicle that are being introduced to reduce pollution and improve gas mileage.

Electric vehicles are also at the forefront of automotive technology. Their introduction has turned a mechanic's job from mostly mechanical work into mostly electrical and computer work. "The mechanics of the future," says Jada, "will have knowledge less like a mechanical engineer and more like an electrician or computer scientist." This trend means that mechanics are learning whole new skill sets, but it also means that exciting new technologies will be available in our cars.

"Currently, there are a lot of amazing new technologies being researched, which will make your car ride significantly safer and make your drive more pleasant and even fun," says Jada. For example, Jada's company is currently researching an electronic sun visor that will dim the windshield of a car depending on the direction and strength of the sun's rays. Her company is also working on a system of cameras that will be able to tell if a driver has fallen asleep at the wheel, wake them up, and keep them from getting into an accident. According to Jada, though her company isn't working on it, the German government is

Learn more about self-driving vehicles.

WHAT IS A SELF-DRIVING VEHICLE?

Scientists are developing cars and other vehicles in which human drivers are never required to take control to safely operate the vehicle. These self-driving vehicles use sensors (technology that collects information) and software to control, navigate, and drive the vehicle. Self-driving vehicles may be autonomous (they use only vehicle sensors to drive), or they may be connected (they use communications systems that allow systems in the vehicle to communicate wirelessly with roadside infrastructure). Self-driving vehicles are also known as autonomous vehicles and driverless vehicles.

At this point, there are no fully autonomous vehicles on the road in the United States. However, partially autonomous vehicles are being introduced. They can manage vehicle speed, steering, and braking under certain conditions. But a driver must still be on hand to take over when the conditions on the road are too demanding for the system.

Some people believe that self-driving cars will reduce the number of accidents, but considerable research and development are still needed before these systems can be completely trusted to replace a human driver. Automotive experts are also concerned with developing self-driving vehicle software that cannot be hacked (taken control of) by criminals to steal the vehicle or make the car crash into other vehicles.

even researching a project that will use a system of cameras, both in cars and on the road, that will take care of most traffic jams!

New technology is constantly in development. The commercial freight truck industry already uses technology that monitors speed and automatically applies the brakes if a driver isn't paying attention or falls asleep. Self-driving vehicles are being developed that may replace human-driven ones—but that will not happen for years.

These new technologies are not too far away. Someone interested in becoming a car mechanic should stay up to date on all of the new technology that is being researched and installed in our cars today. It may very well be the technology future mechanics will have to deal with on a daily basis!

A GROWING FIELD, A SHRINKING NUMBER OF MECHANICS

According to the U.S. Bureau of Labor Statistics, employment for automotive service technicians and mechanics is expected to increase by 6 percent through 2026, about as fast as the average for all other jobs, including those that require a college degree. For anyone who participates in an apprenticeship as a car mechanic or who attends a vocational or technical program, getting a job will be easy over the next few years because of a shortage of mechanics who are skilled enough to work on all these new technologies.

According to Jada, the amount of new technology in a car, especially microprocessors, has been part of the reason behind the current shortage of car mechanics. "These computers keep curious people from checking under their hood," she explains. "You now need another specialized computer to hook up to your car in order to tell whether or not it needs to be repaired. For a trained technician, these specialized computers make it easier to diagnose most problems with your car, especially smaller problems, which are notorious for disappearing as soon as you bring the car in for repairs. But they don't encourage the average Joe—or Jane—to start poking around under the hood."

Ironically, while computers have made diagnosing car problems easier for mechanics, they have also discouraged curious young people from becoming mechanics. "Even though diagnosing problems has become easier," explains Jada, "actually fixing the problems can be much harder unless you are specially trained for these kinds of computers, especially some of the more advanced ones that are coming out today."

Automotive repair and maintenance is quickly turning into a field for highly skilled labor, which means that mechanics both now and in the future will need, above all else, to continue to learn. "But," Jada says, "a lot of this learning still happens on the job. The sooner you get into the automotive workforce, the better prepared you will be once the technology changes!"

DID YOU KNOW?

In 2018, 20 percent of Americans said that they would most likely buy an electric vehicle the next time they bought a car, according to AAA, a federation of motor clubs throughout North America that has 58 million members. This was an increase from the 15 percent who said they would do so in 2017.

IN CLOSING

While automobile technology continues to grow, change, become more complex, and, as a result, make the job of a car mechanic more challenging, it is also one of the reasons that being a car mechanic today is so exciting!

Repairing and maintaining today's cars requires a very interesting mix of skills. You need both the ability to work with traditional machines and expertise in digital information technologies and computers. While many careers are available for someone who wants to work with machines (machinists, engineers, electricians) or computers (web designers, information technology specialists, software programmers), very few careers offer the chance to work with both.

The people interviewed in this book are intelligent and passionate. They work in a career that's quickly changing, which means they are constantly striving to stay abreast of the latest technology. They decided that earning a bachelor's degree wasn't the right choice for them—not because they are unintelligent or lack ambition (have dreams of being successful in life). Instead, they took another path to get what they wanted: a good salary, the chance to advance, and fulfilling work. Earning a bachelor's degree may be the best option for you. Or another road might be your path to success. Either way, consider every option and be open to all possibilities. Be willing to learn and work hard, no matter where life takes you!

WISE WORDS

"To accomplish great things we must not only act, but also dream; not only plan, but also believe."
—*Anatole France, French poet, journalist, and novelist*

"Happiness is not in the mere possession of money; it lies in the joy of achievement, in the thrill of creative effort."
—*Franklin D. Roosevelt, thirty-second president of the United States*

"Commit yourself to your own success and follow the steps required to achieve it."
—*Steve Maraboli, motivational speaker and author*

RESEARCH PROJECT

Learn more about advanced vehicles and fuels by visiting www.nrel.gov/workingwithus/advanced-vehicles-fuels.html and other websites. How will they change the work of auto mechanics? Write a one-page report that details your findings.

TEXT-DEPENDENT QUESTIONS

1. What are hybrid cars?
2. Why is there a shortage of auto mechanics?
3. What is a self-driving car?

SERIES GLOSSARY
OF KEY TERMS

accreditation: The process of being evaluated and approved by a governing body as providing excellent coursework, products, or services. Quality college and university educational programs are accredited.

application materials: Items, such as a cover letter, resume, and letters of recommendation, that one provides to employers when applying for a job or an internship.

apprenticeship: A formal training program that combines classroom instruction and supervised practical experience. Apprentices are paid a salary that increases as they obtain experience.

associate's degree: A degree that requires a two-year course of study after high school.

bachelor's degree: A degree that requires a four-year course of study after high school.

certificate: A credential that shows a person has completed specialized education, passed a test, and met other requirements to qualify for work in a career or industry. College certificate programs typically last six months to a year.

certification: A credential that one earns by passing a test and meeting other requirements. Certified workers have a better chance of landing a job than those who are not certified. They also often earn higher salaries than those who are not certified.

community college: A private or public two-year college that awards certificates and associates degrees.

consultant: An experienced professional who is self-employed and provides expertise about a particular subject.

cover letter: A one-page letter in which a job seeker summarizes their educational and professional background, skills, and achievements, as well as states their interest in a job.

doctoral degree: A degree that is awarded to an individual who completes two or three additional years of education after earning a master's degree. It s also known as a **doctorate**.

for-profit business: One that seeks to earn money for its owners.

fringe benefits: A payment or non-financial benefit that is given to a worker in addition to salary. These consist of cash bonuses for good work, paid vacations and sick days, and health and life insurance.

information interview: The process of interviewing a person about their career, whether in person, by phone, online, or by email.

internship: A paid or unpaid learning opportunity in which a student works at a business to obtain experience for anywhere from a few weeks to a year.

job interview: A phone, internet, or in-person meeting in which a job applicant presents their credentials to a hiring manager.

job shadowing: The process of following a worker around while they do their job, with the goal of learning more about a particular career and building one's network.

licensing: Official permission that is granted by a government agency to a person in a particular field (nursing, engineering, etc.) to practice in their profession. Licensing requirements typically involve meeting educational and experience requirements, and sometimes passing a test.

master's degree: A two-year, graduate-level degree that is earned after a student first completes a four-year bachelor's degree.

mentor: An experienced professional who provides advice to a student or inexperienced worker (mentee) regarding personal and career development.

minimum wage: The minimum amount that a worker can be paid by law.

nonprofit organization: A group that uses any profits it generates to advance its stated goals (protecting the environment, helping the homeless, etc.). It is not a corporation or other for-profit business.

professional association: An organization that is founded by a group of people who have the same career (engineers, professional hackers, scientists, etc.) or who work in the same industry (information technology, health care, etc.).

professional network: Friends, family, coworkers, former teachers, and others who can help you find a job.

recruiting firm: A company that matches job seekers with job openings.

registered apprenticeship: A program that meets standards of fairness, safety, and training established by the U.S. government or local governments.

resume: A formal summary of one's educational and work experience that is submitted to a potential employer.

salary: Money one receives for doing work.

scholarship: Money that is awarded to students to pay for college and other types of education; it does not have to be paid back.

self-employed: Working for oneself as a small business owner, rather than for a corporation or other employer. Self-employed people must generate their own income and provide their own fringe benefits (such as health insurance).

soft skills: Personal abilities that people need to develop to be successful on the job—communication, work ethic, teamwork, decision-making, positivity, time management, flexibility, problem-solving, critical thinking, conflict resolution, and other skills and traits.

technical college: A public or private college that offers two- or four-year programs in practical subjects, such as the trades, information technology, applied sciences, agriculture, and engineering.

union: An organization that seeks to gain better wages, benefits, and working conditions for its members. Also called a **labor union** or **trade union**.

work-life balance: A healthy balance of time spent on the job and time spent with family and on leisure activities.

FURTHER READING & INTERNET RESOURCES

FURTHER READING

Derrick, Martin and Simon Clay. *Million Dollar Classics: The World's Most Expensive Cars*. New York: Chartwell Books, 2017.

Heptinstall, Simon. *Cars: A Complete History*. San Diego: Thunder Bay Press, 2014.

Roach, Martin and Neil Waterman. *The Science of Supercars: The Technology That Powers the Greatest Cars in the World*. Richmond Hill, ON, Canada: Firefly Books, 2018.

Zettwoch, Dan. *Science Comics: Cars: Engines That Move You*. New York: First Second, 2019.

INTERNET RESOURCES

www.nrel.gov/workingwithus/advanced-vehicles-fuels.html This website from the National Renewable Energy Laboratory is a great place to learn about advanced vehicles and fuels.

www.bls.gov/ooh/installation-maintenance-and-repair/automotive-service-technicians-and-mechanics.htm This section of the *Occupational Outlook Handbook* features information on job duties, educational requirements, salaries, and the employment outlook for automotive service technicians and mechanics.

www.bls.gov/ooh/installation-maintenance-and-repair/automotivebody-and-glass-repairers.htm This section of the *Occupational Outlook Handbook* offers information on work responsibilities, personal skills, educational requirements, and the job outlook for automotive body and glass repairers.

www.ucsusa.org/clean-vehicles/how-self-driving-cars-work Visit this website to learn how self-driving cars work.

EDUCATIONAL VIDEO LINKS

Chapter 1
Learn why it's a great time to become an auto mechanic:
http://x-qr.net/1G8w

Chapter 2
An auto mechanic discusses a typical day on the job:
http://x-qr.net/1FUp

Chapter 4
Learn more about opportunities for women in the
automotive industry: http://x-qr.net/1F4f

Chapter 5
Learn what happens during an automotive service
competition at SkillsUSA: http://x-qr.net/1Gae

Chapter 6
Learn more about self-driving vehicles: http://x-qr.net/1Fzg

INDEX

Summer Ignite Program, 55
suspension, 34

T

U

V

W

AUTHOR BIOGRAPHIES

Andrew Morkes has been a writer and editor for more than twenty-five years. He is the author of more than twenty-five books about college planning and careers, including all of the titles in this series, many titles in the Careers in the Building Trades series, the *Vault Career Guide to Social Media*, and *They Teach That in College!?: A Resource Guide to More Than 100 Interesting College Majors*, which was selected as one of the best books of the year by the library journal *Voice of Youth Advocates*. He is also the author and publisher of "The Morkes Report: College and Career Planning Trends" blog.

Christie Marlowe lives in Binghamton, New York, where she works as a writer and web designer. She has a degree in literature, cares strongly about the environment, and spends three or more nights a week wailing on her Telecaster.

PHOTO CREDITS

Cover: AdobeStock; Front Matter: Shutterstock; Chapter 1: © Industryviews | Dreamstime.com, © Kunal Sehrawat | Dreamstime.com, © Lawrence Weslowski Jr | Dreamstime.com, © Robert Kneschke | Dreamstime.com, © Coloradonative | Dreamstime.com, © Robwilson39 | Dreamstime.com, © Monkey Business Images | Dreamstime.com; Chapter 2: © Tom Wang | Dreamstime.com, © Dmitry Kalinovsky | Dreamstime.com, © Ikonoklastfotografie | Dreamstime.com, © Viktor Bondar | Dreamstime.com, © U.S. Department of Energy, © Monkey Business Images | Dreamstime.com, © Christa Leigh Turski | Dreamstime.com; Chapter 3: © Srki66 | Dreamstime.com (tools, main), © Norgal | Dreamstime.com (air filter), © Kelpfish | Dreamstime.com (battery), © Uldis Bindris | Dreamstime.com (dashboard), © Richard Gunion | Dreamstime.com (fuel cell), © Renato Borlaza | Dreamstime.com (rust); Chapter 4: © Auremar | Dreamstime.com, © Hongqi Zhang (aka Michael Zhang) | Dreamstime.com, © Photographerlondon | Dreamstime.com, © Auremar | Dreamstime.com, © Kurhan | Dreamstime.com, © Photographerlondon | Dreamstime.com, © Odua | Dreamstime.com; Chapter 5: © Dragonimages | Dreamstime.com, © Tyler Olson | Dreamstime.com, © Rainer Klotz | Dreamstime.com, © Andrew Morkes, © Andrew Morkes, © Sergei Butorin | Dreamstime.com, © U.S. Army Educational Outreach Program, © Ben Schonewille | Dreamstime.com; Chapter 6: © Kurhan | Dreamstime.com, © Tktktk | Dreamstime.com, © Jingaiping | Dreamstime.com, © Monkey Business Images | Dreamstime.com, © Iakov Filimonov | Dreamstime.com